SHA... ROCK

Written by Ben Hulme-Cross
Illustrated by Luke Finlayson

Chris didn't remember how Shark Rock had got its name. Maybe it was because it looked like a big shark fin.

Maybe it was because of all the sharks that hunted there!

Chris was in his boat, fishing near the cliffs. He saw some young kids swimming around Shark Rock.

Didn't they understand how risky it was? Was that a fin poking out of the waves? He called out to the kids, but they didn't hear.

The wind was blowing his cries back into the cliffs. Chris pulled up his small anchor. Then he pulled the cord to start the boat.

Nothing happened!
He looked back at Shark Rock.
The kids were still swimming.

And what was that, closer to the kids this time? Was it the fin? He called out again, but the wind was even stronger now.

He tried the cord again.
This time the boat jumped into life.

Chris pointed the boat at Shark Rock and began to cut across the waves. He couldn't see the fin. Where was it?

Just then, one of the kids saw him.

Chris waved his arms about.

The kid pointed at him and smiled.

Chris cut the motor.

He saw the dark fin shape out of the corner of his eye.

"Quick!" he called. "Get in the boat!"

They all swam over and Chris helped them in.

"What about Kay?" one of them said. "She's on the rock."

Chris looked over at the rock. Kay was standing on the rock, pulling on a thin rope.

Chris gasped.

There on the end of the rope was a toy boat with a dark blue sail. The sail looked just like a shark fin!